80 Great Things about Being 80

By

Pat Cook and Friends

International Standard Book Number 13: 978-1-60452-030-9
International Standard Book Number 10: 1-60452-030-2

Library of Congress Control Number: 2009904401

BluewaterPress LLC
52 Tuscan Way Ste 202-309
Saint Augustine, FL 32092
http://bluewaterpress.com

This book may be purchased online at -

http://bluewaterpress.com/80things
or on
amazon.com

To the Reader –

Just so you'll know:

...the pictures of people included are, for the most part, not of the ones who contributed the quote. Some brave souls posed for the less glamorous photos.

...there are several pictures and quotes involving grandchildren...these reflect the place of grandchildren in the lives of many 80-year-olds.

...we can't say "Thanks" enough to those who contributed their ideas and to the models who helped demonstrate them. A list of these true photo friends is provided at the end of the book.

Many thanks go to my son, Professor Thomas R. Cook, of Keene State College, in New Hampshire, for most of the photos in this book. His suggestions and advice were invaluable. Thanks, too, to daughter-in-law, Kelly, and their sons Ben and Walter, along with my son Kevin, daughter-in-law, Pam, and their children, Cal and Lily, all helping with photo suggestions, especially the ones most off-the-wall.

Thanks go to the Keene, NH, fire department for accommodation above the call of duty and to the CCC of Indianapolis for keeping my computer alive and well. Thanks to Carolyn Welch for continued good advice and to Nancy O'Dell for proofreading par excellence and continued support.

My endeavors are always dedicated to Arthur B. Cook.

A great thing about being 80 is...

1. ...being surrounded by grandchildren.

....Carolyn Welch

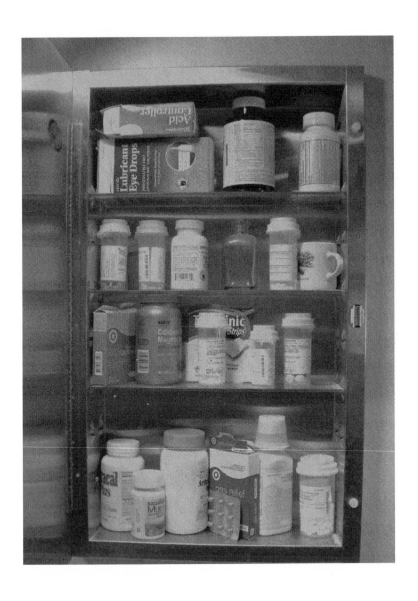

2. ...becoming as fascinated as my friends with stories of their operations and bodily functions.

...Jim Sunkes

3 ...having secrets be really safe with friends, because they probably won't remember them, anyway.

...Pauline Shaver

4 ...not needing an alarm clock any more...we
   don't even need a clock!

                              ...Betty and Van Eller

5 ...having people call at 10:00 in the morning and ask, "Did I wake you?"

...Diann Lorber

6   ...isn't it nice that wrinkles don't hurt?

...Phyllis Barrett

7   ...seeing how much younger I look (I think) than those pictures of my grandmother at 80.

...Sue Roll

8 ...life may not always have turned out the way I planned, but I'm still dancing.

...Marie Thomas

9 ...now if I bowl close to my age, everyone thinks it's terrific.

...Dee Conner

10 ...having grandchildren run to my
outstretched arms.

...Dee Todd

11 ...most days, the weightiest decision I have
to make is whether to have soup or salad.

...Ellen Healey

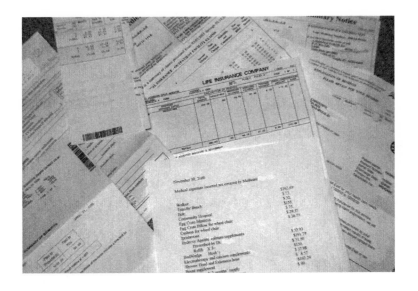

12 ...knowing that all those health care
premiums are beginning to pay off.

...Ann Sunkes

13 ...treating my grandchildren to their hearts'
contents, and knowing a few indulgences
won't hurt them.

...Marge Strack

14 ...it doesn't take much to please me – just feeling safe and secure when I get to dry sidewalk after walking over an icy patch...

...Marge Stevens

15 ...there's an old saying, "Life isn't about waiting for the storm to pass; it's about learning to dance in the rain."

...Nancy Thomas

16 ...senior discounts...those are good things.

...Pat Unger

17...having people my own age around who remember some of the same things I do.

...Patti Horrigan

18 ...I'm not considered disrespectful to be
wearing tennis shoes anywhere, any time.

...Bonnie Parker

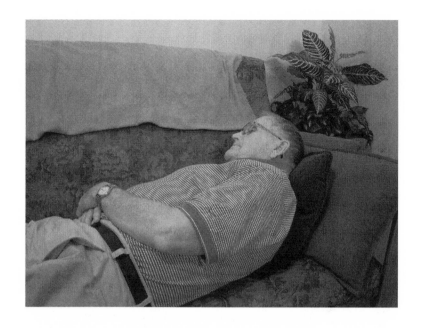

19...naps - don't we all love them?

...Charlie Todd

20...not lying about my age any more...now I
    brag about it!

...Marlane Tisdale

21 ...youth and exuberance are wonderful, but age and experience can pay off, too!

...Suzie Areddy Schenk

22 ...getting closer and closer to being able to shoot my age in golf.

...Martha Erickson

23 ...not having to hold my stomach in – who cares?

...Rita O'Connor

24 ...seeing my grandchildren grow from adorable babies and tots into delightful PEOPLE.

...Carolyn Davis

25 ...saying, "Thank you, Lord"...We didn't think
we'd make it this far.

...Patty and Ray Mayer

26 ...it's like a roll of toilet paper. The closer you get to the end, the faster it goes!

...Joan Vondersaar

27...when I look in the mirror without my
   glasses, I look just like I did 50 years ago!

...Ginny Watson

28 ...a lot of the struggles of life have already happened, so now it's all down hill and easy.

...Pam Lorber

29 ...being proud of having served in World War II.

...Ray Parker

30 ...I used to watch my mother knit and
    crochet and wonder if I'd ever have that kind
    of time...and now I do!

...Jo Dearing

31 ...while girls today think Brad Pitt is cute, the
movie actors of our youth were rugged and
handsome.

...Conrad Lane

32 ...although I've experienced just about
everything, I can still find guidelines for
whatever might happen.

...Greg O'Dell

33 ...I don't ever have to buy eyeliner again...my eyelids sag so much I can't draw a line on them.

...Judy Ramsey

34 ...bedtime is whenever I fall asleep in my
reclining chair.

...Ginny Compton

35 ...I'm so practical, if I fall, I wonder what else
I can do while I'm down there.

...Pattie Gray

36...if I decide to skip my "senior" classes to play golf, I won't get sent to the principal's office.

...Elizabeth Clark

37...I'm not really expected to RUN anywhere...
  what a relief!

...Annie Dillon

38 ... "One of these days" has disappeared from
my vocabulary.

...Jeanne Ravaux-Newburg

39 ...we grew up with great music...Yes, we had
   our "Three Little Fishies" and "Mairsy Dotes,"
   but we also had "Stardust," "As Time Goes
   By," "In the Mood..."

...Betty Bartz

40 ...as little girls we had a steady stream
of strong, independent, career-minded
role models like Amelia Earhart, Eleanor
Roosevelt, and Katharine Hepburn to show
us endless possibilities...they're still role
models.

...Martha Lane

41 ...the candles on my birthday cake could
  heat the house.

...Marianne Weaver

42 ...hearing from grade-school friends of 70
years ago and meeting them for lunch.

...Bob Stahl

43 ...I'm learning to master the computer, and
know that a hard drive doesn't mean bad
road conditions, and that a byte doesn't
always mean having lunch.

...Nancy Blackmun

44 ...if they say I'm "off my rocker," they just mean I'm heading for the mall.

...Richard Miller

45 ...here are three of the best...

...Dot Ahlers

46 ...after 80, every day is gravy...some days it's a little lumpier than others, but gravy is gravy.

...Rosie Eagan

47 ...so what if my wild oats have turned to
  bran and prunes...I like bran and prunes.

...Mary Ann Barnes

48 ...we were blessed to have had the dancing of
Eleanor Powell and Ginger Rogers and Fred
Astaire...Home video lets us enjoy them all
over again.

...Malcolm Woodworth

49...while the "Baby on Board" sign was good in its day, I like this new one, too.

...Pat Garvin

50 ...I don't worry about gas prices because I
   don't HAVE to go anywhere.

...Nina Innis

51 ...I can always say the lines in my face are
   "laugh lines."

...Jan Snodgrass

52 ...books and magazines come in BIG PRINT...
thank you!

...David Parker

53 ...I can read at 3:00 o'clock in the morning
    if I want to ...and I know I won't be tired
    tomorrow, 'cause I can sleep in.

...Barb Mattingly

54...I'm finishing my puzzle and my cuppa tea
and looking at my flowers at 11 AM.

...M. Louise D. Barnett

55 ...in graduate school I used a slide rule...now I punch numbers into a calculator. I'm glad I lived to see that!

...Edi Otterson-Powell

56 ...I've learned a few things in my life, but so far they haven't helped me one damned bit.

...Judy Henderson

57...we are still lucky to be able to see and hear Nelson Eddy and Jeanette MacDonald, who can exemplify "true romance."

...James A. Moore

58 ...the older I get, the better I was.

...David Powell

59...I'm finally the "Grande Dame" (or is it the "Damn Gran"?)

...Sue DeBoer

60 ...my exercise program can be just to lean over and feed the dog.

...Charles Bravard

61 ...now I have the time to sit on my deck,
unhurried, and savor the beauty of Nature and
feel I am a part of the life around me.

...John Stafford

62 ...we look at what we've collected
throughout our lives, and enjoy thinking of

where and when and how and why we bought
them.

...Lela and Gene Smyth

63 ...having more time to do my "Ups": Wake Up; Dress Up; Reach Up (for something higher); Stand Up (for what I believe in); Look Up (old friends); Lift Up (those who need help).

...Debbie and Dave Duncan

64 ...we can spend more time in church, catching up on our "knee-mail..."

...Steve and Monica Parker

65 ...the satisfaction of knowing I've had a successful professional and personal life.

...Sister Francesca Thompson, O.S.F.

66 ...we don't have to wonder how we'll look
when we get old(er).

...Bill Barrett and Bob Eagan

67 ...I don't have to worry about tooth decay any more.

...Kay Sanders

68 ...I've always enjoyed driving our covered bridges...seeing them and hearing them; there are still a few around...grey and creaky...kind of like me.

...Betty Boxell Carey

I've never been so comfortable before.

Oh, I'm so glad that I'm not young anymore.

69 ...singing along with Maurice Chevalier, "I'm Glad I'm Not Young Anymore." (Forgot the lyrics? Go online or rent "Gigi" and watch it again.)

...Shirley and Bill Connette

70 ...I can re-read books that I loved, because I don't remember the endings.

...Susie Douglass

71 ...it doesn't matter as much if the mail carrier or delivery person sees me in mismatched clothing...I dress for comfort, not style.

...Marg Allison

72 ...we don't worry about the weeds in the garden or yard...dust doesn't bother us at all, especially when we have good books to read.

...Ann and Tom Thibault

73 ...my old clothes are suddenly "vintage," and my out-of-style furniture has become collectible.

...Nancy O'Dell

74 ...if a kid gets sassy, I can say, "When were you alive that I wasn't?"

...Betty Bogeman

75 ...I don't cry because it's over...I smile because it happened!

...Kathy Morrow

76 ...I can e-mail friends around the world and I have a reply within minutes – amazing!

...Diane Koehler

77 ...I've lived to see old crank-up phones turn into cell phones...I knew we'd catch up with Dick Tracy!

...Bob Morrow

78 ...I can tell my grandchildren stories about their parents, and if I hear about it later, I can always claim I don't remember telling them...

...Susan Bravard

79 ...I was born on the day Lindbergh took 33½ hours to fly to France...now I can make that trip in 7 hours watching a movie and eating a leisurely lunch...wow!

...Pat Cook

80 ... "One must wait until evening to see how splendid the day has been."

...Usually attributed to Sophocles -
submitted by Walt and Becky Wykes

These are the names of people whose photographs appeared in this book:

Jack Abernethy
Kara Abernethy
Meg Abernethy
Grace Ahlers
Maggie Ahlers
Sam Ahlers
M. Louise D. Barnett
Col. (Ret.) Robert Barnett
Bill Barrett
Phyllis Barrett
Larry Benaquist
Dee Conner
Ben Cook
Kelly Cook
Pat Cook
Tom Cook
Walter Cook

Bob Eagan
Rosie Eagan
Judy Henderson
Eric Mattson
Patty Mayer
Grace Newport
Nancy O'Dell
Ray Parker
Charlie Todd
Dee Todd
Ginny Watson
Bobby Welch
Carolyn Welch
Clare Welch
Molly Welch
Tess Welch

Made in the USA
Columbia, SC
18 June 2018